MW01116373

# The Pain of Healing

## Samantha Camargo

Copyright ©2022 Samantha Camargo
All Rights Reserved

# Contents

If you've ever felt like you can't go on
and you feel like you've been healing
forever and things will never get better,

*I made this for you.*

I've been where you are and although
it was extremely hard I made it through
and I know you can too.

# Layers

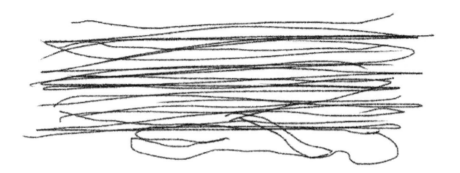

1111

It feels like your soul left you.
You feel empty
and like you can't go on,
but you can make it through this.
One breath at a time, you will.

I'm so tired, but I'm scared of trying
to go to sleep because I'm afraid
it's really going to hit me hard in
the moments before I fall asleep,
with nothing to distract me from
what I'm feeling.

– I miss you so much.

It didn't hit me that life
would have to go on without you,
until I went to bed and realized
tomorrow I will have to wake up

*and you still won't be here.*

I would always try to stop myself from crying
because I hated crying, but this pain
that I'm feeling now hurts so much
I actually want to cry
because then maybe
I could release the pain.

But I've been crying so much
that nothing will come out anymore
and it hurts more than anything
I've ever felt before. I want to cry.
I want to release my pain,
but no tears will come out
and I can feel it
starting to drown me.

The hardest thing wasn't the pain I felt.

The hardest thing was thinking I needed
to move past the grief and be happy already.
The most painful thing was people expecting me
to have picked myself up from the fall,
expecting me to have healed,
while I was still on the ground,
the blood not even finished

pouring

out.

If I had every trace of you
erased from my mind,
my heart would still
ache for you.

He wanted to give her
all of his love so badly,

*he left nothing for himself.*

It's scary how one small smile
can easily hide all of the sadness
you feel inside because most people
will see the smile and ignore
the emptiness in your eyes.

After you passed,
months passed.
November came
December came,
Christmas came,
family came,
and when they left,
the emptiness.

During the day was easier,
not because the emptiness left.
It never left,
but with the noise of the day
it was more of a whisper
and in the quiet of the night
it screamed for my attention.

It's been two months now.

They say it gets easier as time passes,
and in a way it does because life goes on
and it sweeps you up and takes you with it,
moving you from one moment to the next,
one day to the next, one month to the next.

Even when you don't want to and
your body feels limp and lifeless,
life will carry you.

And suddenly it's been 2 months
and the night it happened you didn't think
you could make it through another second,
let alone another day, but somehow you did.
And it gets easier because you allow life to
move you along, in hopes that one day you'll
find the fire inside of you again.

One day you'll find the fuel and the passion
to bring your body back to life and move
yourself, instead of letting life push you along
from one day to the next.

After you passed,
I couldn't feel you anymore.
I tried so hard to,
but couldn't feel anything.

The first time I felt you again
was running in the park
when I looked up and saw a tree
moving with the breeze.

So, I searched for you in nature.
I went hiking and I stopped
on an empty trail
because my body was too heavy
with grief.

I needed a release.

I looked up at the sky,
at the trees framing the sun.
I closed my eyes
and the tears escaped.
I felt so much pain,
but I also felt numb.
Filled with so much grief,
but empty all at once.

I had cut my hair because
I wanted to feel different.
I wanted to be someone else,
someone who didn't miss you...
but I still missed you

and I learned
you can't fast forward
through grief.

We go through so many feelings,
but sometimes it feels as if
we're only present in the sad ones.

You know how chains get tangled,
I mean really tangled...
so much that it seems
impossible to untangle?

The trauma felt like that.

He felt buried in chains.
Overwhelmed,
trying to figure out
how to get free.
He got so tired... so very tired...
trying to untangle it all.
He just wanted it to end.

But his soul whispered,
this is not who you are...
you are not the painful things
that happened to you.

You don't need to carry it with you.
Take it off. Let it go,
before it gets so heavy
that you try to pass it on.

And so he stopped trying to untangle
the endless chains around him,
he took them off, whispered,

*"this is not me."*

He was buried,
but he had always been free.

You try so hard
not to hurt anyone,
but why don't you care
you are hurting yourself?

*You don't deserve this pain.*

From the pain,
she needs a release,
but her mind whispers
her worth will decrease
if she lets the tears
ruin her mask of perfection.
She cannot let them.

With a smile
and her tears kept inside,
behind the mask
she hides.

When you lose someone,
it can open your heart,
but if you're not careful
it can also close it.

It can make you love more openly,
urging you to share your love
with all of the people in your life
as often as you can,
while you are still able to.

But it can also make you want to
close yourself off from the world,
making you cautious
with who you share your love,
as if you don't have much left to give

*and I'm trying so hard to keep mine open.*

I want to give so much love to everyone..
but I feel so empty.

– I want to feel my love again.

3 months later

...

and it hits me.
You're not here
you're still not here
it hits me so hard
I can't breathe
I can't see
I can only feel
you

It's been 3 months now.

I look in the mirror
and I can't see myself anymore.
I look in my eyes and I cannot
see love; they are
empty
and it hurts so much.

But one day,
I will transform
this pain into love,
into so much love.

*I promise you.*

I wish I had showed you
how much I loved you
every second of every day.

I wish I hadn't taken for granted
as many moments as I did.

I don't know how else to explain it
except that I felt something leave my body,
as if my soul could not take
how much pain my body was in
and left immediately.

It took the life out of me
and in that moment
I had no desire to take it back.

I just want to be able to hold you again.
I want so badly to be able to feel you
physically in my arms.

I'm waiting for the day
when I can feel you in my soul,
and my body will no longer ache
to be able to touch you,
to feel your warmth.

I'm waiting for the day
the numbness will fade away,
and I will be able to feel you again.

You came
and cut all the flowers,
but when the struggle
came to grow
you left.

Don't make it your home,
feeling worthless and alone.
Learn, grow, and remember

*you were always enough*
*even if they didn't know.*

The ocean of tears
put out the fire
in his soul

I wonder how many things
I've hidden in my mind
to protect my heart
from acknowledging
the pain of it.

– When I uncover it,
the healing can begin.

I held the speaker to my chest
and started to cry again.
I hugged the speaker so tight.
I felt as if my heart was gone
and I was desperately trying
to replace it with the music I held.

Can you imagine having your home violated,
feeling as if your soul was just shattered,
being traumatized and feeling as if
your whole world will never be the same..
and then being told it's your fault?

Feeling broken
and then being
*crushed*
by those words?

It's been 4 months now.

I look in the mirror,
and I can start to see myself again.
I look in my eyes and they no longer look
empty.
I can see the pain is still there,
but now I can see so much love
trying its hardest to break through
and I've been trying my hardest
not to break down, but maybe I need to;
maybe I need to break.

*Maybe that is how the love gets through.*

Who knew the words
*"I love you"*
could break your heart.

So much pain
shaking their bones
how much more
can they take
together,
but feeling
so alone

They had always held hands,
but now they had to let go
as they clutched their chests
a pain deep in their hearts

They both fell
so hard,
so far
apart

They each blamed the other
for the pain they couldn't bear

"Why weren't you there?"

They couldn't see,
blinded by the pain
that brought them to their knees

How could one comfort the other
as they mourned
How could they hold them
when their hands were full of thorns

I'm not as strong as you think I am.

I'm still healing.
The blood has finally stopped pouring out,
but the scar is forming.
And I'm trying my best not to reopen it,
but sometimes I accidentally touch it
and I can feel the pain piercing my skin again.
It's still fresh so sometimes the pain hits me
all over again.. but new skin is growing.
And soon it won't hurt me at all.

*But until then, please let me heal.*

After losing you, I felt guilty whenever
I found myself able to feel happy again
and guilty whenever I found myself
feeling sad, as if I should be over it already.

This feeling is a prison.
A prison I keep myself in.

And I'm the only one who can set myself free.
By learning how to not feel guilty
for feeling, for being human.

*Why do I feel guilty for being human?*

I wish someone had told me how fast
time would pass and to wake up instead
of walking through half my life not truly
present. Walking through life stuck in
my head instead of living in my body,
experiencing every single second and being
grateful for it all. But then I think even if
someone had tried to tell me this, I probably
wouldn't have really listened. Maybe learning
how to live in the present moment and
learning how to appreciate every experience
we have in our bodies is something we all
have to learn on our own, in our own time.

She vowed to never need anyone
because in her mind, needing
caused suffering.

To need someone,
as our bodies need oxygen,
meant she needed them simply
to continue to breathe
and if they left they would
take her last breath with them.

*And so she vowed*
*to never let anyone*
*become her oxygen.*

I'm fine. Actually, I'm more than fine.
I'm happy and everything is okay.
But then, my mind wanders and
I end up thinking of you, and suddenly
my whole body aches and I wonder if
I had been numbing myself so I wouldn't
have to feel the pain of missing you this
whole time and I wonder how long
I will have to continue to numb myself
and I wonder how much longer it will hurt,
and when I will be able to think of you
and feel happy for the memories we shared
instead of sad that you're no longer here.

*And I wonder if you ever really do heal
from losing someone.*

It's been 5 months now...

and I still think about you every day.
Some days I think I've healed,
while other days the wound opens up
deeper than before.

*And every single day,*
I still miss you.

She thought she had found
a home in his soul,
but he just wanted warm bodies
because he was tired of the cold.

It had nothing to do with you.
You are enough
and you always were enough.
She had covered her heart with ice,
numbed herself.

*How could she feel love for you...*
*when she couldn't even for herself?*

When those words left his lips,
they surrounded her
unguarded heart
and crushed it.

– It was over in an instant.

A week after, I acted as if I had
put myself back together again,
so quickly, so easily.

I even almost fooled myself,
but then I saw a photo of myself.

The truth was in my eyes
and the way they made my body
look vacant as if there were
no signs of life.

When you cry, you cover your face
and "sorry" spills from your lips.
You try to wipe away your tears
as you apologize still
as if you've been taught
it's shameful to feel.

I crave for people to be there for me.
I know it's only human to want someone
to be there for you when you're having
a hard time, but why do I crave it?
Maybe it's because I am desperately
trying to avoid being there for myself
and I want anything but to be alone
with my own thoughts.

*I will stop needing people to be there for me.*
*I will learn how to also be there for myself.*

It's been 6 months now. Half a year.

And I still remember the day you passed.
I remember feeling empty and I thought
about how excruciatingly empty it will feel
as the days go on without you and turn into
weeks, then months, then years.

And that emptiness is still there
and it is excruciating,
but I am trying to fill it up.

*I am trying to fill it up.*

Healing is hard
and you have to
work on it day by day
even though
you'll want to hide
and pretend
everything is okay.

I don't know if I could ever
love myself as much as I love others
because I would break myself
in order to heal everyone I love.

*But how can I help them if I'm broken?*

When you feel as if your relationship is falling
apart and it's gone so dark that neither of
you can find the spark you once both felt in the
beginning, the fire that awoke your
entire being... take the time to find out
if it's because you two are growing apart
or growing together.

Find out if you two are falling deeper and deeper
only to find nothing at the end of it
or if you both are making your way to find
a deeper love for yourselves and each other.

It's like you shot me and you helped me
take the bullet out but there were still
little pieces of it left inside of me
and when I tried to dig them all out
so I could heal, you told me I need to stop
touching the wound so I can heal faster.
But I'm trying to get all the pieces out
before it seeps into my bloodstream,
entering my veins, consuming me..

– I don't want to lose myself.

I felt a heaviness in my head
and when that was gone,
it was replaced with
a hollowness in my chest.

Don't allow other people's low places
to become your home.

It's been 7 months now and I can't help
thinking how your birthday would be in
3 days and how I wish you could be here
so I could celebrate you being alive, but
you're not and I feel a bit numb. But today,
instead of drowning in regret, I will choose
to be present. I will choose to celebrate you
and enjoy every moment of my life. I will
choose to live my life to the fullest and I
will love to the fullest and I will choose to
be happy. I will celebrate that I got the
chance to have you in my life instead of
dwelling on the fact you're gone. I will try
to remember that even though physically
you're gone, you will always be with me,
in memories, in my heart, and in the
voice that tells me I deserve to be loved
unconditionally, I deserve to be happy,

*and I am worthy of all the good things
in my life.*

Whenever I feel like I need a fresh start,
I cut my hair. Maybe it's because I want
to run away from myself and leave who
I was behind me. Or maybe it's because
I don't want to be the person who lost you
anymore. Maybe I want to be someone
who doesn't know how it feels to have
loved someone with their entire soul
and to feel this type of emptiness that
I don't know how to fill up. Maybe I am
running away from myself because I'm
scared of being this person who feels as
if I don't have enough love to give anymore.
But maybe I'm not running away from myself.

Maybe I'm running towards who I really am,
while leaving behind the parts of myself that
have been holding me back.

– And maybe when I get there, my soul will
feel full again.

I feel so empty.

But I am grateful
because of all the love
you filled me up with
while you were with me.

But now
I feel so empty.
I feel so empty.
I feel so empty.

*I feel so empty.*

I wasn't always closed off.
I once allowed myself to leave
my heart completely open.
I let all my love flow to one person
and once they were gone I felt empty.
I began to close off my heart,
so no more love could escape.
But I didn't realize I boarded it up
before I could let any love back in,
including my own.

*I ended up harming myself
trying to protect myself.*

You are feeling weak and afraid
and that means
you are strong and you are brave.
What you are going through is excruciating,

*yet here you are still trying each day.*

It's been 8 months now
and I miss you more than ever.
I feel you in the sky. I feel you
in my favorite songs. I feel so numb,
but at the same time.. I feel so alive.

I was afraid to go back
to my everyday life
because that meant
it was true..
life would have to
go on without you.

"You're always so happy,
but are you really okay?"
she asked
and I watched in horror
as my mask nodded
and smiled back.

I couldn't even cry
because I didn't want
anyone to hear me.

*The silence is painful.*

Once you've been hurt by someone
you loved and trusted with your life,
your whole life feels like a lie and what
once was filled with so much love,
is now filled with so much pain.

He learned that's what happens
when you're in a toxic environment..
you begin to think the problem is you,
not the environment.

It's hard for them to believe you
when you tell them they're worth it,
after they've heard they are worthless
for so long. But help remind them

*they are so much more
than they've been told.*

It's been a year now...

and I cannot believe I am writing those words.
I can still remember the day you passed and
I remember thinking how I'd wake up and you
wouldn't be there and how much it would hurt
each day I woke up and you weren't there.

I can remember that day so vividly and it's
hard to wrap my mind around the fact that
the day before I lost you, you were here. Just
the day before, you were there, so close to me.
And now, a year later, I feel so far from you.

Now that it's been a year,
it hurts less and it hurts more.
As the days go by, I feel as if
the wound is healing,
and yet growing deeper

*because I miss you more and more each day.*

When you wake up from a dream
that makes you so sad you start crying,
years after they've passed,
it doesn't mean you haven't healed.

–It just means you loved them
so very much and you miss them.

I've made myself so busy
I have no time to cry
no time to process
my emotions
every day I'm just
going through the motions
I have no time for the grief
it's taken piece after piece
left me with no peace
running on no sleep
avoiding my feelings
afraid to go deep

*everyone keeps leaving*
*I have no time to weep*

It seemed to be out of nowhere when
she started crying and she was asked,
"What made you remember him?"

But they didn't know
she could never forget him.

He was not constantly on her mind,
but the memory of him was always there,
somewhere inside of her.

The memories were etched onto her soul,
a part of her forever.

Have you ever been through something
so painful, so life changing that once it's
over you feel like you've grown years in
a matter of days?

You've never experienced growing pains
physically, in your body,
but you realize now you've experienced it
through your soul.

Generation after generation,
the trauma was passed on...
and here you are lying underneath it all.

*No wonder it feels so heavy.*

We're taught to care more about
appearances than how we feel
and so we focus more on an illusion
than what is real.

*We stay on the surface*
*instead of going deep*
*to heal.*

You'd be surprised how many people hide
how they truly feel... how we put on a mask...
a permanent smile... afraid if we show that
we're not okay... no one would care.

*So we cry in the shower.*
*And no one ever knows.*

Healing is hard.
But so is constantly,
desperately trying
to hold yourself
together.

Trauma isn't always caused by one big event.
It can be multiple events that may seem small
to the observer, but can feel as heavy as the
world

*to the one carrying it.*

Instead of dealing with the pain,
we passed around blame
like a hot potato.
When it got to us,
it burned us with shame
so we kept passing it around
and things never changed.

you feel layer after layer pile on
you're not sure how much more
you can take
how much longer
before you break

# Undone

Grief is so heavy
and death does not wait
until you're ready...
even while you're healing
it can take and take and take
even while you're kneeling,
on the floor,
begging, pleading,
"no more.
this is all my heart can take
*there is nothing left to break*"

Over and over, you lied...
I'm lying here
... shattered on the floor
my trust lies...
can't sleep, wide eyed

What he feared all along happens.
He exposes his heart to her
only to have her walk away,
as if his soul is not worth loving.

They give you nothing
and you say, "take all of me."
They tear you down
and you sit, full of apologies.
They make you feel worthless
and you still think they are worth it
but when will you see,

*you are what's important*

You broke me and
I tried to put myself
back together,
but somehow
I still fall apart
at the slightest touch

When I got the text, I cried so loudly
and so much because I immediately felt so
much pain in my body, pouring out.
I covered my face with the top of my shirt
as if somehow that could protect me..

When you were alive you made me
ceramics and when you passed I
started looking for them. I looked
for them desperately and quickly
lost hope, thinking I had given
them away.

When I found them, I lost it.
I started crying,
feeling celebratory and sad
because I felt as if it was
the only thing left of you I had.

I miss your smile and your gentle eyes
I miss the safe feeling of your bed
with you lying by my side.

You never minded how quiet I was.
You always made me feel safe and loved.
You let me hide in the shadows where
I wanted to be and by doing that you
made me feel seen.

Grief can weigh you down
making you feel so heavy
you could sink into the ground.

But it can also make you feel so light
like you're floating in the air
Nothing feels real and nothing feels right

When I was little,
I was scared of my grandma dying
because I thought she was so much older
than me and thought that meant she was
going to die soon so I cherished every moment
I got to spend with her but when I got older,
I took her for granted, not because I didn't care,
but because I had gotten caught up

*and thought she would always be there.*

What happens when everyone's
asking you for a life vest
when you're struggling to stay afloat?

When you passed,
I felt like time stood still
and all of us stopped moving,
staying with you.

But as time passed...
I feel like everyone
started moving again...
and they're all walking forward,
able to move on... and they think
I'm right there with them,
but I'm not

and I want to be able
to move on, but
I'm still standing still,
holding onto you.

Maybe we feel dead inside
because we are suffocating
our souls
and when we do things
that make us feel free

*we are letting them breathe.*

After what you did to me,
you don't get to say you loved me.
You used me, betrayed me
and you almost broke me,
but you did not love me.

Instead of holding my heart
with your bare soul,
you crushed it
with your bare hands.

What's worse than suffering?
*Everyone else denying you are.*

They deny your pain
because they're too afraid
to face their own.

What you want most
is connection

Genuine connections.

But what you fear most
is allowing people past
the wall you've built
to protect yourself.

And you won't get
what you want most
until your craving
for connection
overpowers your fear
of opening up.

When will you realize
the wall you've built
is the only thing
keeping you from
what you want most..

The phones come out
with the smiles and stares.
They're recording my life
fall apart
but do they care?
From my suffering,
are they entertained?
As they watch,
can they see me?

*Can they see my pain?*

Denying someone else's pain
doesn't stop them from feeling it.

Denying another's suffering
helps create more of it

When someone says
they've been hurt,
they're in pain,
they are suffering

instead of having compassion
and asking,

"What can I do to help you?"

We demand them,
*"prove it."*

As he reached for death,
he felt a pull in his chest.
He saw a little boy's face.

Everyone had abandoned him.

He could not be like the rest.
He decided to take care of him.
He was all he had left.

She felt so much pain as they were driving back and she looked out the window, crying... and she wished no one would ever have to feel this pain that she was feeling now.

She thought that maybe she couldn't prevent it, but at least she could show them they could get through it... that they could feel all this pain and still heal from it...

*and that it would be worth it.*

You promised you wouldn't leave
when things get hard,
but when I was crying, on my knees,
you didn't stay.

At my lowest, you ran away.

You watched him drown
and the waves attack.
Now he swims across oceans
and you want him back.

If you've been cheated on,
please don't give up on love.
They crushed your heart,
but it was never because
your heart was not worth loving.

Sometimes we treat other's hearts
as if they are our own
and if we're hurting inside,
we can end up hurting others.

Understanding this doesn't
make it justifiable.

It is heartbreaking.
It is cruel.
It is life wrecking
and it is not okay.
But, it's important
to understand
that even though it has
affected you so deeply,
it had nothing to do with you.

*You are enough and*
*you always have been.*

They passed you the poison.
It's in your veins.
But you can heal from it.
You can help break this cycle of pain.

Don't tell them you love them
if your love can be taken back
so easily,
as if it was never real
if your love disappears
when their body changes,
as if love is something you see
rather than feel

Don't tell them you love them
if you never asked if anything
was bothering them
if they were feeling stressed
or feeling low
if you never bothered to know

Don't tell them you love them
if you never saw in their eyes,
the pain
but instead left them
because their looks changed
and your love no longer remained

I realized your intention was never
to use your hands to hold me,
but to manipulate me.

"You aren't enough,"
the mind whispers.

*But the soul knows the truth.*

Pulling
"I love you"
out of my mouth
is a struggle

and once it's out
it stings
with the memory of the past.

Those three tiny words
have brought so much pain;
it would take three lifetimes
to explain.

Samantha Camargo

You are a dream
and you love
and you care
and you're right there
in front of me
And I stare
but I can't see
because I'm still
stuck in a nightmare

Now the anger comes so easily
it's almost like a reflex
once the words leave the tip of my tongue
I can taste the regret
I look at my eyes in the mirror
and I can't see any of me left

The anger comes so easily now
and I really just don't know how
to feel anything else
without falling apart
without breaking down

It's a bandage
to a deep pain
I want to heal
I'm tired
of anger
being all I feel

She fought and she fought and she fought,
until she finally let down her defenses
and loved instead.

Exhaustion protected me.
I only went to bed
if I could instantly fall asleep,
whether that would be at 2 or 3
and with no time to think
it didn't hurt to go to sleep.

Samantha Camargo

I don't want to forget you,
but I don't know how to
think about you
without it hurting...

It hurts my heart
whenever I start
to think of going on
with you gone

*it feels so wrong*

I keep her clothes in a box.
I don't open it because
I don't want her scent to get lost.
It's sealed completely;
I wasn't ready for her to leave me.
I wasn't ready to let her go.
How much I love her, I know she knows
but it doesn't take away the grief I feel..
it doesn't take away how it doesn't feel real..
it doesn't take away the time I'll need to heal.

I keep her clothes in a box
but slowly, I know
I'll pry open the seal.
Slowly, I know
I'll be able to heal.

I used to visualize my future
every day
but after you were gone,
it only brought pain.

you've become numb,
completely undone
it's finally broken you
you've lost. it's won

# Bare

How do I let go of the hurting?
My mind is constantly searching
for answers to release the pain,
but it remains the same.

How do I let go
of this feeling
that I'm worthless,
that I'm nothing?
How do I feel
something
else...

They say time will tell
but it's been years
and I'm not doing so well...
How do I let go of what happened
when my mind grasps so tightly?
I feel trapped and
can't see a way out
I don't know how
to stop
the thoughts...

But each day, I am trying
and it's been years
I've felt like I'm dying...
But one day, I promise

*I will be thriving.*

His mind made him feel like the pain
was held in his soul, his heart
and every day he could feel it
tearing him apart.
He couldn't find the button
where he could press restart,
get rid of the past
and have a fresh start.
The mind can play tricks,
be the greatest illusionist.
But the soul never quits.
The mind can bury the truth
until it's hidden it.
But the soul can't stay buried
no matter how much pain we carry
and when we rise from the dirt,
from all the pain and the hurt
it might feel like a struggle,
it might feel like a fight.
But sometimes, that's what it takes
to reach the light
and when we reach the surface,
we realize the light had always been inside.
But sometimes the mind hides...
numbs us with lies,
makes us forget what will always reside
inside
and with each breath, he tries.
Even when he feels buried, he shines.
People see and he helps them breathe
by being alive, by being a seed
of hope.

It's one thing after the other
and life doesn't feel real.
It feels like you're constantly
struggling, pushing yourself uphill
but you can make it through this.

– You can and you will.

Your body doesn't feel like home because
the traumas live in your mind on replay.

It's not your fault
and you are not alone.
The traumas rewire your brain
until you no longer think or feel the same.

There is no shame in asking for help.
*There are strangers in your home.*

When we had it up to here
and were tired of the tears,
of waiting for things to get better
we found strength in knowing
if things never would
at least we could,

*we could get better.*

In this moment,
I feel I am barely hanging on.
I am burning out. I am fading.
I want to sleep better. I want to eat better.
I want to exercise regularly.
I want to take better care of my body
and my health. I want to be present.
I want to live moment by moment and to not
be afraid to really feel every single moment.
I want to free my mind. I want to go to sleep
feeling peace in my soul and wake up feeling
fully alive. I want to feel my soul. I want to
feel love and I want to feel it overflowing
through every pore to everything and
everyone I cross paths with.

*I never wanted to die.*
*I've wanted to come back to life.*

Protect your healing.

Some might not understand
because they don't see you're bleeding.
They can't see what you're feeling.
They don't see the pain.

*Keep on trying every single day.*
*Don't let them stand in your way.*

The trauma makes you feel
as if you are in a horror movie
making nightmares feel real,
seeing things in the dark that aren't there,
always looking over your shoulder,
feeling at peace is rare
whenever things are starting to get better,
it makes you feel as if things could never.

But this is all wiring that came out of trauma.
Your life is not a horror or a drama.
You can regain control over your brain.
You can stop feeling this loss of self
that is making you feel
like you're going insane.
You are not in a movie
that needs a rewrite;
you are in real life,
a life you can change,
where you can feel safe.

Where your mind makes you feel
there is a knife always lurking,
always hidden
there is actually a beautiful,
bright life that wants you

*to live it.*

She was on the brink of falling apart,
holding on by a thread
trying so hard not to go over the edge;
he held her
and she completely shattered.
He helped remind her she mattered.
It wasn't anything he said;
he simply held a space
for her to feel safe,
a place she could break and crumble
and know this is not the end.

He didn't know how much longer
he could put on a "strong" face
covering up his pain,
then she held him
and he fell apart
in the safety
of her arms.

You gave me a space
where I could break
and I could ache,
without looking at me
like I was broken.

Do you ever think of yourself
when you were younger?

I think of her
and wonder
what she would think
if she saw me today,
Would she see how
jaded I've become?
Would she go for a hug
and flinch at the touch?
Would she wonder how much
it took to break me?
*Would she hate me?*
Would she wonder how things
could've went so wrong?
Would she look at me and wonder
how long...
it's been since I've been this way?

But I remember..
every step, every day,
she's been with me.
She understands.
She knows..
and it makes me feel
less alone.

The silent suffering
from thinking
of all the ways
it was your fault
can be deadly.
You can't get it
out of your head
because it was
so sudden
and you weren't
ready.

Don't let the grief
and the guilt
eat you alive.
It wasn't your fault.
It was their time.
They love you
and the only thing
they wish
could've changed
was being able
to say goodbye.

I hope you feel better soon,
but if it's not soon,
I hope you know
you can get through
whatever
you're going through

*and it will be worth it.*

I thought healing myself would take weeks
and then months started to pass. I told myself
something was wrong with me if I hadn't
healed within a year. Each day felt so long
and agonizing, but somehow the time moved
so fast. A year passed, and then another, and
then two more after that. I'm still healing
but I'm starting to become a lot more present.
I'm starting to move on from the past and
I'm no longer afraid of how long it will last.

*I'm feeling more like myself again and*
*I'm starting to remember how it feels to laugh.*

I'm learning how to be easier on myself.
I'm learning how to allow myself to be happy.

*I'm still learning and that's okay.*

Time spent healing is not wasted time.
*It is so important for your existence.*

Music saved them.

Whenever they couldn't imagine
feeling anything but despair,
they would listen to music.

Music that reminded them
of what kept them going.
Music that made them
*feel something.*
Music that touched their soul.
Music that made them feel alive.
Music that made them think of the future
and how the future would be filled with
the same feelings the music made them feel.

In this moment, I am thinking of you
and for the first time I don't feel sad.
I feel as if you're with me.

You're gone, but somehow you're still here.
I feel your support and your love.
I feel you helping me overcome my fears.

Samantha Camargo

It's been almost 3 years now
and it still hurts just the same.
The difference is I'm stronger now;
I can overcome this pain.

She entered her heart
and heard a whisper

*"You are safe here"*

How can you feel empty
when you are so filled with love?

You've only forgotten
*you are love.*

When my heart tried to break,
I held it together
with paper and a pen.

Stop pretending. Start mending.

You deserve to be the kind of happy
you always pretend to be.
Stop pretending everything is okay
and take the time to heal.

It will be hard.
*It will also be worth it.*

Good things don't come *out of* the trauma.
Good things come *after* the trauma,
not because of the people or events that caused it,
but because of yourself.

– The trauma was part of your destruction,
not your resilience or your growth.

Standing up is so powerful
because you are standing in their way
of things remaining the same.
As long as you keep standing up,
things will change.

Every breath you take makes a difference.
Imagine what your actions will do.

*What kind of difference do you want to make?*

Maybe you're scared to acknowledge
the sparks inside of you
because you've been burned badly,
but it's okay to feel again.

For the longest time,
I saw myself as a bad person.
You don't know
how much it meant to me
when you looked at me
and could see the good.

You are a lotus.

It doesn't matter if millions
of people walk by you
and only see mud.

*You are a lotus.*

I see your insecurities, your uniqueness,
your pain, your passions, your anger, your love,
your fears, your dreams, your struggles,
your strengths... and maybe you can only
see the "bad" things right now, but I hope
one day soon you can see all the good too.

Take off all the conditioning.
Take off all the defenses.
Take off all the things
you've been taught you need
and show me your soul.

My pain and my love
sat side by side,
holding hands.

I struggled to let go,
to be set free of my pain.

I fought so hard
until I felt
I had nothing left
to give.

I thought to myself
how love is so weak;
it cannot win a fight.

And I realized
that is not what love
is meant to do.

And my love
took my pain
by both hands
and embraced it.

And as I
embraced my pain,
I released it.

Grief puts the memories on replay,
filling your mind,
making you wish you could rewind..
*But what if we did that starting today?*
What if we took the time
to replay them before..
while there is still time to make more.

Why did it still hurt if you had done
everything you could to protect yourself,
not letting anyone past your defenses?

*You thought you were building a fortress,*
*but you had built a prison.*

Maybe I'm not breaking down..
Maybe this is what opening up
feels like after being hurt so badly.

*I am not breaking, but my walls are.*

The people you will want in your life
are those who love you for your soul,
not just your body.

Samantha Camargo

Don't let anyone
make you feel ashamed
of your grief or your pain
saying "he's just a dog,
so it's not the same"
or "you weren't close to them,
so why do you feel this way?"

It might be something they
can't understand right now
no matter how much
you try to explain,
but it does not change
how you feel;
them not understanding
does not make it any less real.

If you know someone is grieving,
please allow them time to grieve.
Allow them time to heal.
Don't rush them to feel better.
Make them feel safe, reminding them
it's okay to feel however they feel.

I feel better, but also the same.
Sometimes I feel the pain leaving...
Sometimes I feel it trying to stay,
making itself at home
under my skin and in my bones
when I'm with others and when I'm alone.
It doesn't matter when.
Sometimes it leaves
and tries to come back in
and I wonder if it will ever end...
But each time, I heal and mend.
My body is starting to feel like my own;
the pain comes and I know how to let it go

You miss who you used to be
but who you are now
deserves to be loved too.

Your name is just a name now. Memories no
longer rush back, pouring through my body,
flooding my mind, drowning my senses,
when I hear your name. My heart no longer
wants to jump out of my chest to escape
the sting and it's no longer hard to breathe.

*Your name is just a name now. And I am free.*

You are not too emotional just because
you are finally allowing yourself to truly feel
everything you always tried to hide.

You are not a burden just because you are sad
and not covering it up with a smile.
Even if you've been sad for what seems like
a long time, you are still not a burden.

And you deserve people in your life who will
love you even when you are feeling sad
or unworthy of love. They will love you through
it all because they truly love you and not just
who you are when you are happy.

We support things that help
protect ourselves or our beliefs,
but we should ask ourselves whether
we are harming others to protect our beliefs.

Sometimes we judge out of fear,
but to connect, choose love over fear.

The weight of healing the world is so heavy.
It seems impossible to achieve,
but what if we just tried carrying ourselves,
being a safe space for anyone looking for
peace.

Allow them to be vulnerable around you.
Make them feel safe to share
their deepest thoughts with you.
Teach them that feeling things deeply
is not a weakness, but a strength.

It takes courage to feel love
because you are also opening
yourself up to the possibility
of feeling unbearable pain.

But you clutch your chest and bear it.

You feel the pain, but you have also
awakened a power that obliterates
the pain and you feel all your
courage, strength, and power
pulsating in your chest.

When I met you,
it felt as if I had discovered fire.

I was so excited. Everything felt surreal. There was a whole new world to discover. You shone light. I felt alive, so exhilarated. You radiated warmth. I felt warm, so comfortable. But, I was cautious not to get too close because I didn't want to get hurt. I didn't want to get burned. My excitement overcame my fears and I played with my discovery. I threw myself into the unknown; I reveled, I celebrated, I explored. I let my guard down and allowed myself to be vulnerable. I was full of joy. I danced and danced and danced as if the moment I was in was eternal and nothing could touch me. I danced so close to the fire. I could feel the heat against my skin. And I let it touch me. It hurt so much. It was too much. And it was too late. The fire consumed me. It was so painful. It was agony. It took the breath out of me. I could feel it take my soul, my very essence. It took my life. But I emerged and I discovered I was still alive. The fire had not touched me. It had only burned. It had burned everything I wasn't and I came out, not damaged, not broken, but whole and more alive than ever before. My love overcame my fears. And I discovered fire cannot burn fire. Light cannot put out light. When light meets more light, it illuminates the darkness. And I discovered this when I met you.

*There is nothing to fear.*

You don't have to shrink yourself. It's safe to
take up space. You deserve to take up space.
You are enough. You are worthy of having
a voice. You are worthy of thriving and
inspiring others to do the same. Deep down
you know that your soul has been waiting
for you to. The world has been waiting for
you to. Souls have been waiting for you.
You can handle anything that comes your
way. It's time for you to light a pathway
to help others find their way.

–We've been waiting for this day.

And finally he accepted feeling lost
and let happiness find him.

Sometimes you don't realize
how bad it's gotten
until things start to get better.

It's been 5 years now
and I miss you still.
I've accepted the fact
I always will,
but it's no longer
a sudden wave
crashing over me
until I can't breathe.

It's no longer
an urgent, aching
painfully breaking
beat in my heart.

It's more of a gentle beat
of a heart at peace,
a heart that had to
put itself back together
piece by aching piece.

I'm not grateful I went through it.
I'm grateful I overcame it.

There is pain, but there's also a lot of
healing and growth and love
and I hope you can feel all of that too.

When it happened, it completely broke me
and I thought I could never love again,
but here I am struck with the overwhelming
feeling of loving you.

Looking at them,
so excited and passionate about their life,
they reminded me of how I used to be.

They helped me remember
it's possible to be like that again
and that feeling this empty is not me.

She was overflowing with radiance
and being in her presence,
it washed over me
making me feel that maybe
things could be alright
and that somehow they will be.

He jumped up and down so excited, so high.
He was a living example of loving life.
He was a living, breathing form of light.
He was a reminder of what it feels like to be
alive.

As I stared at her, dancing around her room
filled with so much love and joy and wonder,
I hoped there wouldn't come a day where I will
have to remind her of the joy she used to feel
when she was little, but if I have to I will be there,

*without a doubt I will be there.*

I think trauma makes our lives pass us by,
pulling us inward, making us stuck in our
heads thinking of the past or trying to
protect ourselves in the future and healing
is about releasing ourselves, opening up and
being able to be present with life

*and trusting that you will be okay*
*no matter what happens.*

You're never too late, not even if you think you are and you don't think you can believe otherwise. It's not too late because at any moment you can still change that thought and you can change your actions.

*As long as you are alive,*
*things can change and there is time.*

Based off the past years, we know we can't
depend on life being gentle to us. Instead,
I hope you are gentle with yourself. I hope
you see how hard you've worked... even if
you feel as if you didn't. You've been getting
by each and every day and I know how much
strength that takes. You've been through so
much these past years, through so much pain
and so many tears. Yet, you are still here.

And every second, minute, hour, day, week,
month, and year after year after year...
I will forever be grateful you are still here.

We can't expect life to be gentle to us,
so let's do what we can
and be gentle to ourselves.

Existing is enough
and even during the hardest times,
any second can be filled with love.

Since you were a child, you grew up
in this place you call home
but you were told
"this is not your home"
and you were shown
all the ways you are different
and you listened and listened
and started to feel like you don't belong
but they were so wrong
I wish I could've told you what they didn't say
this is your home and you deserve to feel safe
they buried you in fear and pain
they made you think
"Everyone thinks I'm strange"
they made you feel so alone
and made you forget what matters most.

We are all made of skin and bones
and I wish you were shown
you are not strange.
I wish you were shown
you deserve more than this pain
and I wish you had known
what they didn't say;
you are an incredible soul

*and wherever you are,*
*you will always be home.*

After going through what he'd been through,
he didn't want to be praised for being tough.

*He just wanted to be held and loved.*

What happened to us was not
inspiring or life changing.

It was heartbreaking
and almost life taking.
It was overwhelming and grave,
making our bodies cave.

Weighed down with dread
we couldn't lift ourselves out of bed.
Nightmares were alive in our heads

but somehow we escaped
from days that tried
to take our lives
somehow we kept going
somehow we survived
and not only that,
we actually thrived

*What happened couldn't break us*
*no matter how hard it tried.*

No matter how long you've felt
empty, broken, lost, or afraid,
wanting to escape
it's not too late.

Even if you've felt
like this for years
as long as you are here,
as long as you are alive,

*there is still time.*

If you try breaking me over and over,
I'll lose myself, lose hope, and lose
everything I thought I was. But even
after losing everything, I won't give up.
I will keep standing, no matter how many times
you knock me off my feet. There is something
inside of me you can never touch.

*You have no power over me.*

I was buried, layers on top of layers.
I couldn't get out. There was no way.
I lost myself in a labyrinth of pain.
But I found it was never an ending
meant to be feared, but a pathway
leading me to find
what had always been there
beyond the barriers:
my soul,

bare.

Thank you for being here.

If you are reading this, I am so grateful
for you and grateful that you are here.

You being here
alive
is so important
and I hope you
always remember that.

Also, thank you to my husband, Josue, for
helping me design my cover and for telling
everyone I would be writing books before
I even thought I could.

Thank you to my parents and all of my family
for your constant love and support.

Thank you.

If you want to read the book while listening to
a playlist of songs I put together for this book,
you can find it on my Spotify:

@samxcamargo

Made in the USA
Middletown, DE
26 September 2023

39455474R00110